Basic Concepts Series

How Maps and Globes Help Us
How Charts and Drawings Help Us

How People Live in Canada
How People Live in Central America
How People Live in Mexico
How People Live in Brazil

How People Live in the Middle East
How People Live in Africa
How People Live in China
How People Live in India
How People Live in Japan

How People Live in the U.S.S.R.
How People Live in Australia

How Man Began
How People Lived in Ancient Greece and Rome
How People Lived in the Middle Ages
How Our Government Began

How Documents Preserve Freedom
How Schools Aid Democracy
How Money and Credit Help Us
How the American Economic System Functions
How Immigrants Contributed to Our Culture

How People

Live in the Middle East

By **HOWARD O. YATES**

Bureau of Elementary Curriculum Development, New York

Illustrated by **BERTHOLD TIEDEMANN**

BENEFIC PRESS publishing division Beckley-Cardy Co.

CHICAGO Atlanta, Long Beach, Dallas, Portland

Contents

Library of Congress
Number 62-13999

Title page photo: Publix
Contents page photo: 'Round the World

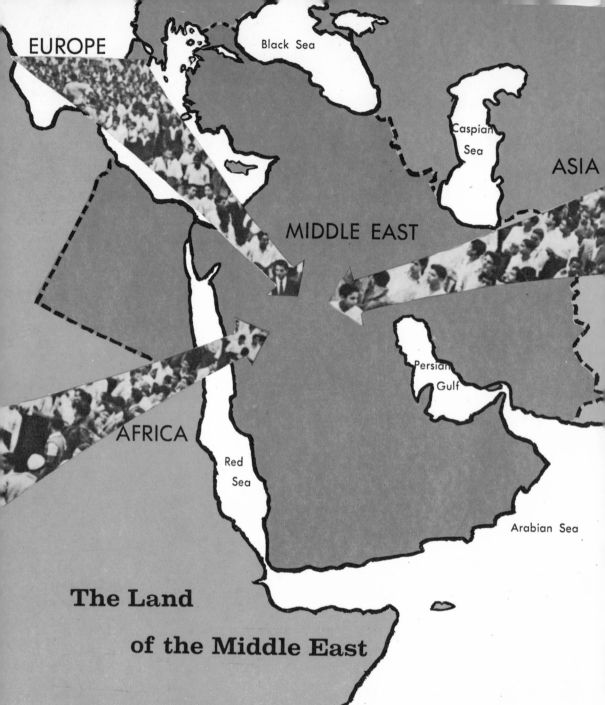

EUROPE

Black Sea

Caspian Sea

ASIA

MIDDLE EAST

AFRICA

Persian Gulf

Red Sea

Arabian Sea

The Land
of the Middle East

This is the Middle East—"crossroads" of the world. The Middle East is an area of land located at the meeting point of three continents, Europe, Africa, and Asia. A <u>continent</u> is one of the seven largest bodies of land into which the earth is divided.

6

For many years, the Middle East has been a crossroads for people going back and forth from Europe and Asia. Traders of long ago crossed the Middle East as they brought silks and spices from Asia to the people of Europe. One route was all overland. Camels and other animals carried the trading goods on their backs. The other two routes were partly over land and partly over water. The goods were taken by boat as far as possible. 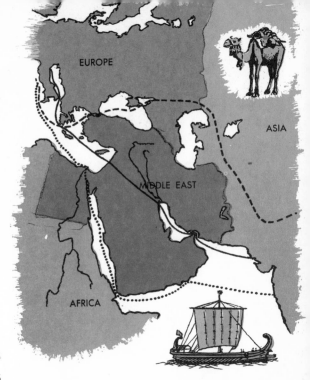 They were carried by animals across the land. A number of important bodies of water surround the Middle East. The shores of the Mediterranean Sea, the Aegean Sea, the Black Sea, the Caspian Sea, the Persian Gulf, the Arabian Sea, and the Red Sea all touch parts of the Middle East.

Today, ships still carry trading goods between Europe and Asia. They cross the Middle East as they pass through the Suez Canal. This narrow waterway was cut through the land that separated the Mediterranean Sea from the Red Sea. Now ships can carry goods all the way from Asia to Europe. Goods need not be taken overland part way.

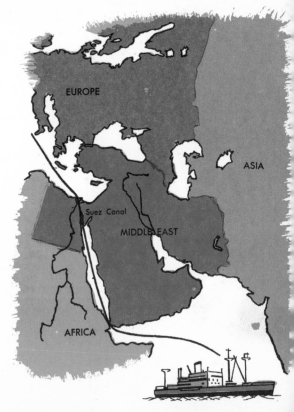

In more recent years, the large and powerful nations of the world have discovered another reason for coming to the Middle East. Their reason for coming is to get oil.

It is believed that more than half of the world's entire store of oil is to be found in the Middle East.

Where is the Middle East?

The map shows that most of the Middle East lies on the Asian Continent. A smaller part lies in the northeast corner of Africa. A very small part reaches into the continent of Europe.

How large is the Middle East?

The Middle East may be considered fairly large. It includes an area almost as large as the United States. Much of the Middle East lies farther south than the United States.

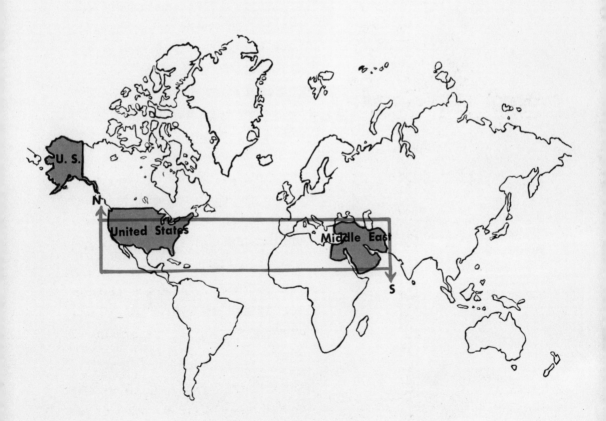

Wide World

United Press International

Kaufmann and Fabry

What kind of land does the Middle East have?

In general, the land features of the Middle East include mountains in the north and along the seacoasts, and plateaus in the other regions. Plateaus are high, mostly flat land areas.

The plateau regions of the central parts of the Middle East are very dry. The mountains along the coasts cut off most of the rain clouds that would bring moisture from the surrounding seas to the plateaus. This lack of moisture causes desert areas and many semi-arid regions in the Middle East. The deserts are very dry, mostly sandy areas where almost no plants at all can live. In the semi-arid regions, the land is poor and dry. Only a few small plants and no trees at all will grow here.

What kind of climate does the Middle East have?

The Middle East has several different kinds of climate. The average yearly weather conditions of a certain region over a period of years make up its climate.

Publix

The northern mountain areas are cool the year round. In some places, the mountains are so cold that people live in these areas only during the spring and summer months. The man in the picture is dressed warmly because of the cool mountain climate.

Along the coasts of the Mediterranean Sea, the summers are hot and dry, and the winters cool and wet. The coast of the Arabian Sea, however, has warm rainy summers, and warm, fairly dry winter seasons.

The semi-arid regions have very hot, dry summers and cold, dry winters.

The desert climate is hot and dry almost all year. In some of the desert areas, it is believed that no rain has ever fallen. In other Middle-East desert areas, it rains only two or three times a year. The rain comes down in torrents and runs off in roaring rivers which soon dry up.

Kaufmann and Fabry

Since most of the Middle East has either a semi-arid or a desert climate, it is easy to see why this area of the world is thought to have a "poor climate."

11

EGYPT

IRAN

JORDAN

IRAQ

SAUDI ARABIA

TURKEY

LEBANON

ISRAEL

SYRIA

What countries are in the Middle East?

Although the Middle East is often thought of as a single area, it is made up of a number of separate countries. In this book, the name "Middle East" will mean the following group of countries: Egypt, Saudi Arabia, Jordan, Syria, Lebanon, Iraq, Iran, Turkey, and Israel.

The small countries of Yemen, Oman, Qatar, Bahrain, and Kuwait along the coasts of Saudi Arabia are also independent nations of the Middle East. Each of these is ruled by a <u>sheik</u>, the chief of an Arabian tribe. The Trucial Coast, also called The United Arab Emirates, is shared by seven sheiks.

Country	Area in square miles	Population	Population density per square mile
EGYPT	386,662	37,519,000	97
IRAN	636,296	33,383,000	52
IRAQ	167,925	11,100,000	66
ISRAEL	7,992	3,356,000	420
JORDAN	37,738	2,739,000	73
LEBANON	4,015	3,401,000	847
SAUDI ARABIA	831,313	8,861,000	11
SYRIA	71,498	7,363,000	103
TURKEY	301,382	39,896,000	132

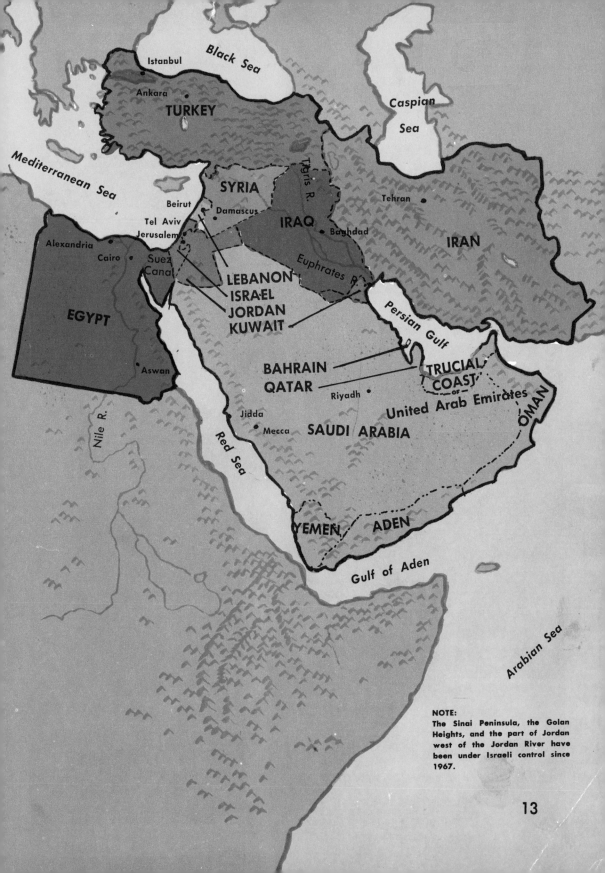

Black Sea

Istanbul

Ankara

TURKEY

Mediterranean Sea

Caspian Sea

SYRIA

Tigris R.

Beirut
Damascus

IRAQ

Tehran

Tel Aviv
Jerusalem

Baghdad

IRAN

Alexandria

Cairo

Suez Canal

Euphrates R.

EGYPT

LEBANON
ISRAEL
JORDAN
KUWAIT

Persian Gulf

BAHRAIN
QATAR

Riyadh

TRUCIAL COAST of
United Arab Emirates

Aswan

Jidda

Mecca

SAUDI ARABIA

OMAN

Nile R.

Red Sea

YEMEN   ADEN

Gulf of Aden

Arabian Sea

NOTE:
The Sinai Peninsula, the Golan
Heights, and the part of Jordan
west of the Jordan River have
been under Israeli control since
1967.

13

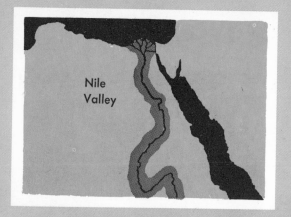

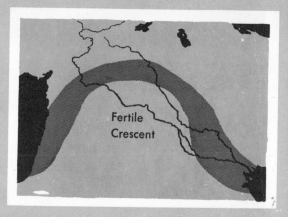

Early Civilizations

Through the years, many different groups of peoples have lived on the earth. We say that some of these groups had civilizations but others did not. The peoples who had civilizations are those who built strong, beautiful buildings; wrote down their thoughts; made laws; and found ways to teach others.

Two important centers of early civilization were in the Middle East. One of these centers was the Nile River Valley. This is a strip of fertile land that lies along each side of the Nile River.

The second center of early civilization was the Fertile Crescent. This area of land lies along the eastern shores of the Mediterranean, curves northward through the present countries of Syria and Iraq, and then follows the Tigris and Euphrates Rivers south to the Persian Gulf.

No one knows exactly why civilization grows in some places and not in others. Fertile soil in these two areas must have helped the ancient peoples living there to develop their civilizations. Here, not everyone was needed to work the land in order to grow enough food for all the people. There were some people left to do the things that make a civilization.

How old is Egyptian civilization?

Written records of Egypt go back as far as 3100 B.C. (before the birth of Christ). About this time, a king named Menes brought a number of small kingdoms together into one country, Egypt. Menes set up a strong government and led his people in building irrigation ditches. These ditches brought the water of the Nile to crops growing along its banks. Irrigation, or a method for bringing water to dry lands, has always been necessary in Egypt. Very little rain falls in Egypt.

During these early days, Egyptian people began using a kind of picture-writing known as hieroglyphics. We have learned much about Egyptian civilization from hieroglyphics carved in stone or written on papyrus. Papyrus was a kind of paper made from reeds growing along the Nile.

When did the Old Kingdom begin?

Beginning with the year 2700 B.C., the history of Egypt is divided into three periods: the Old Kingdom, the Middle Kingdom, and the New Kingdom. The Old Kingdom, beginning in 2700 B.C., is remembered best for its many pyramids. The pyramids are huge, pointed, four-sided monuments made entirely of stone. The Egyptians buried their great kings in the pyramids. The pyramids remain today to remind us of the greatness Egypt once enjoyed.

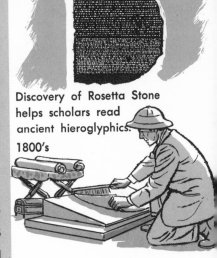

Discovery of Rosetta Stone helps scholars read ancient hieroglyphics. 1800's

Rolls of ancient writings found in Egyptian buildings.

Hieroglyphics first written on papyrus paper in Old Kingdom

Papyrus reeds first made into a kind of paper in Old Kingdom.

Hieroglyphics carved into stone By 3100 B. C.

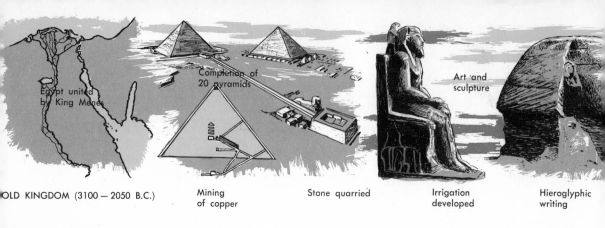

OLD KINGDOM (3100 — 2050 B.C.)

Egypt united by King Menes

Completion of 20 pyramids

Art and sculpture

Mining of copper

Stone quarried

Irrigation developed

Hieroglyphic writing

Many talented artists and sculptors lived during the time of the Old Kingdom. Their works have been found in the pyramids. The great Sphinx, a stone statue with the head of a man and the body of a lion, was also built by Old-Kingdom Egyptians. Many temples were built, for religion was a powerful force in the lives of the ancient Egyptians. They worshipped the sun-god, whom they called "Re."

The Old Kingdom was a period of greatness, but it came to an end after almost seven hundred years. The kings became weak and did not keep order in the country. Finally, the people began fighting among themselves. They did not take care of their irrigation ditches, and the desert sands soon covered the once fertile fields.

When was the Middle Kingdom?

About 2050 B.C., a new line of strong kings gained power in Egypt and made it a strong country again. The little town of Thebes, on the Nile, was the capital. It soon grew to be the most beautiful city in the ancient world.

NEW KINGDOM (1570 — 1090 B.C.)

Palaces and temples of Queen Hatshepsut

Egyptian Empire built

Temple at Ke finished

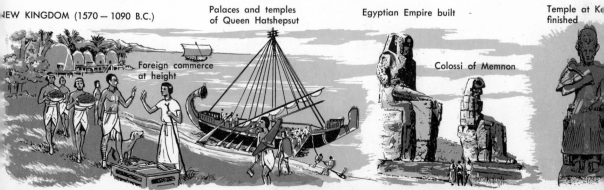

Foreign commerce at height

Colossi of Memnon

at temple
Karnak begun

...LE KINGDOM (2050 — 1570 B.C.)

Trading with
other countries

Irrigation
improved
and extended

Hyksos rule (1730 — 1570 B.C.

During the Middle Kingdom, Egypt enjoyed more than two hundred years of peace and good times. Great irrigation ditches were built. Large paddle-wheel pumps were used to lift the water from the Nile into the ditches.

Egyptian workers made tools, jewelry, pottery, weapons, and many other things. They traded the things they made with people from other lands.

The building of the giant temple at Karnak was begun during this time. This temple was one of the greatest buildings of all time. It was not finished by the people of the Middle Kingdom, however, for while they were still working on it, Egypt was attacked by strong armies.

Savage tribes from the north swept into Egypt about 1800 B.C. These people were called the Hyksos. They were strong fighters, armed with bows and arrows and riding in horse-drawn chariots. The peaceful Egyptians were no match for these skilled warriors. The Hyksos stayed in Egypt for many years, living in camps surrounded by walls of earth.

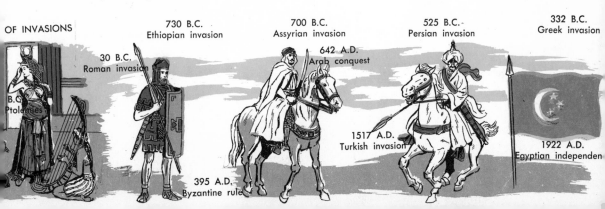

OF INVASIONS

730 B.C.
Ethiopian invasion

700 B.C.
Assyrian invasion

525 B.C.
Persian invasion

332 B.C.
Greek invasion

30 B.C.
Roman invasion

642 A.D.
Arab conquest

...B.C.
Ptolemies

1517 A.D.
Turkish invasion

1922 A.D.
Egyptian independen...

395 A.D.
Byzantine rule

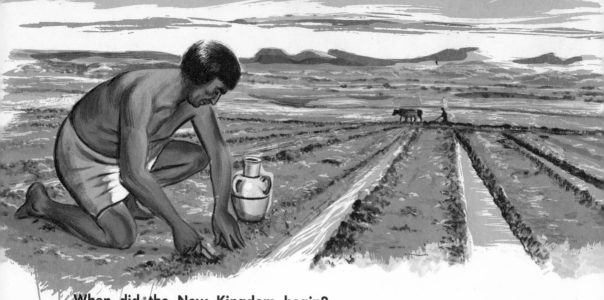

When did the New Kingdom begin?

After long years of living under Hyksos rule, the Egyptians learned the methods of warfare used by the Hyksos. In about the year 1570 B.C., the Hyksos were driven out. Egypt once again became a strong country. The period of the New Kingdom began.

Having learned the art of warfare, the Egyptians began to build an empire; that is, they traveled to other lands to conquer and rule the people living in them. At one time, the Egyptian Empire reached as far as the Tigris-Euphrates Valley. Slaves and riches from other countries were brought to Egypt. The slaves were forced to rebuild old Egyptian temples, to build new ones, and to build huge statues, such as the Colossi at Memnon. The temple at Karnak was finished during this period.

What has happened in Egypt during later years?

After several hundred years of the New Kingdom, the power of Egypt began to decline. Never again did Egypt become a strong country. Beginning with year 730 B.C., Egypt was ruled by many different nations. First came the Ethiopians, then the Assyrians, the Persians, the Greeks, the Romans, the Arabs, and the Turks. Egypt belonged to the Turks until after World War I.

Where was Mesopotamia?

The land which lies between the Tigris and the Euphrates rivers was known to the ancient world as Mesopotamia. Civilization grew up here at about the same time as in Egypt. The first civilized people to live here were the Sumerians, whose capital city was Ur. It is believed that they were the first to use cuneiforms for writing. A <u>cuneiform</u> is a kind of wedge-shaped letter that stands for a word or a part of a word. The Sumerians scratched the cuneiforms into clay tablets.

The Sumerians built irrigation works and used the waters of the Tigris and the Euphrates for the dry lands farther away from the rivers. It is generally believed that the Sumerians invented the wheel.

Who were the Babylonians?

The rule of the Sumerians lasted in the valley of Mesopotamia for several hundred years. Then the people from the city of Babylon became very powerful and captured the whole Tigris-Euphrates area. There were a number of Babylonian kings, but the most famous of all was Hammurabi. Hammurabi was a real leader of his people and was probably the first ruler in history to set down a system of written laws.

SUMERIAN CIVILIZATION

Art

Cuneiform writing

Household items

The wheel

BABYLONIAN CIVILIZATION

Hammurabi's laws

Architecture

After several hundred years of Babylonian rule, Mesopotamia fell to the Assyrians. The Assyrians were a cruel, warlike people who lived at the upper end of the valley. Their capital city was Ninevah. From it, they pushed their control to the Mediterranean Sea and even into Egypt.

One of the Assyrian kings, Sargon II, captured large numbers of Hebrews and brought them to Mesopotamia as slaves. These captives are famous in history as the "lost tribes of Israel."

The people of Mesopotamia suffered greatly under the rule of the Assyrians. The country became poor and the people hungry. No one felt like working in the fields or taking care of the irrigation ditches because the Assyrians took away most of the crops in taxes.

Finally, the king of the Medes and the king of the Chaldeans helped the people of Mesopotamia to drive the Assyrians from their land. Their capital at Ninevah was destroyed, and the Chaldeans set up the second Babylonian kingdom.

What was the Second Babylonian Kingdom?

The most famous king of this period was Nebuchadnezzar. He built many beautiful palaces and temples. The famous "Hanging Gardens of Babylon" were built under his rule. It is said that he built the gardens to please his wife, who came from the hilly country of Persia and was unhappy with the flat lands of Babylonia. There is little left today of these gardens or other Babylonian buildings. The clay bricks of the Babylonians did not last nearly as long as the stone used by Egyptian builders.

The ancient Babylonians spent much time studying the stars. They made maps of the stars and even found five of the nine planets known to man today. Our own way of telling time in minutes and hours is believed to have begun with the people of ancient Babylonia.

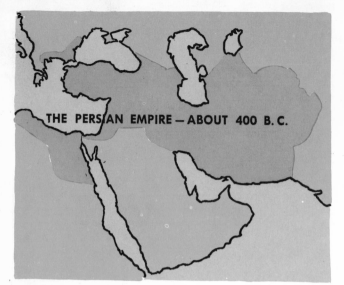

THE PERSIAN EMPIRE — ABOUT 400 B.C.

When did the Persians rule?

The second Babylonian Kingdom did not last long. In 500 B.C., Cyrus, king of the Persians, sent his armies into Babylonia. All the lands of the Middle East were under Persian rule for the next two hundred years. The Persians were strong but fair rulers, and their period of rule was one of peace and happiness for the people of the Middle East.

What is the later history of the Middle East?

Since the time of the Persians, the Middle East has been ruled by many different peoples. First came the Greeks under Alexander the Great. Then came the Romans, who ruled for several hundred years. It was during the rule of the Romans that Christ was born in Bethlehem, a little town in the country of Palestine.

At the time the Roman Empire was falling apart, the Arabs were growing strong under their great leader, Mohammed. Soon the Arabs held all of the Middle East, North Africa, and parts of Europe. A group of warlike people from Asia, called the Seljuk Turks, made war on the Arab lands. They were won over to the Arab religion, however, and were soon part of the Arab people.

The last people to become rulers of the Middle East were the Ottoman Turks. They stayed in control until very recent years. Only since World War I, have Turkey, Iran, Iraq, Syria, Lebanon, Arabia, Jordan, Egypt, and Israel been free countries of the Middle East.

22

GHTS FROM HISTORY

About 2000 B.C.— am's journey naan.

About 1200 B.C.— Exodus to Canaan under Moses' leadership.

About 1500-1200 B.C. — Egyptian exile.

About 1225-1020 B.C. — Nation ruled by judges.

About 1004-586 B.C. — Nation ruled by kings; kingdom divided into Israel and Judah.

The People

of the Middle East

As we have just seen, the story of people in the Middle East is a very old one. In many ways, this story influences the Middle-East peoples of today, in the languages they speak, in their religion, and in their way of life.

Who are the Jews?

The story of the Jews began many centuries ago in the ancient city of Ur in Babylonia. In this city lived a young man known as Abraham. Abraham was unhappy with the religion of his day. The people worshipped many different gods that they carved from stone, gold, or other materials. Abraham believed there was only one God. When he was older, Abraham moved to Canaan, later called Palestine. There he and his family lived and practiced their belief in one God. Some of Abraham's descendants became the Jewish people.

721 B.C. — Assyrian destruction of Israel: "ten lost tribes."

586 B.C. — Babylonian captivity of Judah.

538 B.C. — Return to Palestine.

63 B.C. — Romans ruled the Jews.

70 A.D. — Romans destroyed Jewish holy city, Jerusalem, and Jews lost their country. Many Jews began moving from Palestine.

1897 A.D. — Founding of Zionist Movement and the return of many Jews to Palestine.

1948 A.D. — Establishment of Israel as

Since the time of Abraham, Palestine has been regarded by the Jewish people as their Promised Land. The Promised Land has not always been a happy land for the Jews, however. It has often been a battlefield. From the first ancient days, the Jews fought tribes of other peoples for their right to live in Palestine. For five hundred years, Palestine and her people were under the harsh rule of the Romans. The Arabs and the Turks, in turn, overran and ruled Palestine. During the Middle Ages, Palestine was the battleground for the <u>Crusades</u>, or wars the European Christians fought with the Turks.

Over the long years of fighting, Palestine became a poor and barren country. Rich farmlands became wasted swamps. Once great cities were empty and their buildings falling apart. Most of the Jews left Palestine to live in other parts of the world. Those who stayed were very poor. Arabs made up most of the population. They, too, were poor.

24

Not until 1882 did the Jews of the world again consider making Palestine a national homeland. In that year, a group of European Jews moved to Palestine. This was the beginning of the Zionist Movement, an idea that Palestine should be a Jewish country.

After World War I and World War II, many more Jews began to move to Palestine. The Arabs, however, objected to the idea of Palestine as a Jewish country. They felt it should remain an Arab state. This difference of ideas led to many conflicts and fights between the Jews and the Arabs of the Middle East.

In 1947, the United Nations divided Palestine into two states, Israel to the west, and Jordan to the east. Israel was to be a Jewish country, and Jordan an Arab country. The Jews accepted this plan but the Arabs did not. More fighting resulted between the Jews and Arabs. Finally, in 1948, the Zionists declared Israel an independent state. It had formerly been under the protection of Great Britain. Yet fighting continued until the United Nations ended it in 1949.

-Wide World

The Jews of Israel, with the help of other countries, have been working hard to develop industries and to improve their way of life.

The picture shows two men at work in one of the first Israeli automobile factories in 1948.

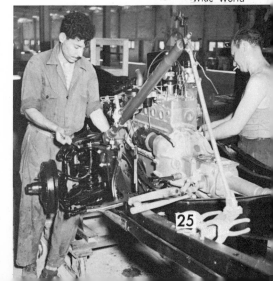

25

Who are the Arabs?

The Arabs are all those people who speak the Arabic language. At one time, the term Arab meant only those people living in Arabia. Over the years, however, these Arabs left the deserts of Arabia to look for more fertile land or to make war on other countries of the Middle East. Today, Syria, Iraq, Egypt, Lebanon, and Jordan are all called Arab countries because the people living in them speak the Arabic language.

Most Arabs are also <u>Moslems</u>, or followers of the Islamic religion. Moslems believe in one God which they call Allah. They believe that Mohammed was the messenger or prophet of God. The sacred book of Islam is the Koran.

Mohammed was born 570 years after the birth of Christ in the Arab city of Mecca. At this time, the Arabs worshipped many gods and spirits. As a young man, Mohammed came into contact with many Jews and Christians. He was influenced by their belief in one God and felt that the practice of his own people was wrong. When he was forty years old, he began to teach Islam and the idea of one God.

At first Mohammed had only a few followers in the city of Mecca. In the year 622, however, Mohammed went to the city of Medina, where many people listened and believed his teachings. He organized his followers into a strong military force and began to spread the Islamic faith "by the sword." That is, he conquered neighboring cities and Arab tribes and won them to the new religion. By the year 632, when Mohammed died, all the peoples of Arabia had accepted Islam. After his death, the Arabs went on to conquer all of the Middle East, North Africa, and parts of Europe.

KORAN

EUROPE

ASIA

THE MOSLEM WORLD

AFRICA

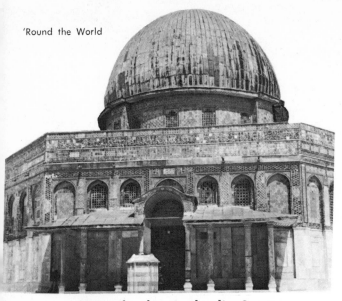

Today, more than ninety percent of all the people of the Middle East are Moslems. They believe that everything that happens is "the will of Allah." If people are sick, hungry, or poor, most Moslems believe it is the will of Allah.

How do the Arabs live?

In the desert areas, the Arabs are organized into tribes, each with a leader called a sheik. These tribes are mostly shepherds who wander over the deserts with their camels, sheep, and goats in search of water and grasslands. They carry their tents and other supplies with them, camping at one place until the grass and water are gone and then moving on to a new place.

Wide World

Arabs living in the more fertile areas are usually farmers, called <u>fellahin</u>. The fellahin live in villages. Their small houses are mud or stone huts.

In the large cities, new modern buildings are replacing many of the old Arab ones. The picture shows a beautiful hotel in a city of the Middle East.

In other sections of the cities, however, old Arab customs are still carried on. Here is the Shourgha Bazaar section in the city of Baghdad, Iraq.

29

How do the Arabs dress?

Some Arabs wear clothing similar to that worn in Europe and in America. These are the few wealthy and educated Arabs and some of those living in the large cities.

United Press International

In the villages and farm areas, however, the Arabs dress the same as Arabs centuries ago. An Arab woman wears a large shawl over her head and shoulders. She often uses the shawl to hide her face when strangers are present. Jewelry also plays an important part in the dress of Arab women.

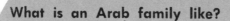

Many Arab men, especially in the farm and desert areas, also wear long robes. They wear long headcloths, held in place by a twisted cord. These cloths protect the people from the burning sand and sun.

What is an Arab family like?

Kaufmann and Fabry

The family is very important in Arab life. The oldest man of the family, usually the grandfather, is the leader. This man's word is law for all his sons and their wives and children. Family groups are large, some having thirty or more members. They all live together in a group of small houses.

Arab women are not considered as important as men. The Arab woman has few rights and must obey her husband or father in all things. Arab children are strictly controlled. They are expected to work from an early age and have little time to play.

How are the Iranians different from other Middle-East peoples?

Iran is not included in the Arab countries of the Middle East because most of the people living there do not speak Arabic. More than half of the Iranians speak the Persian language.

United Press International

There are several small groups of different people living in Iran. These groups all speak their own languages. The largest of these groups is the Kurdish people. These people live in the northwest mountain area of Iran. Many of them live in tribes, wandering through the mountains with their flocks of cattle, sheep, and goats. Many raise excellent horses.

Although most Iranians are Moslems, their way of life differs somewhat from that of the Arab Moslems. Women and children have more freedom and do not have to work so hard.

About three-fourths of the Iranians live in small villages and farm areas. Their houses are small and made of mud-brick. The houses may be built around an open courtyard that has a water pool and a few trees. The water from the pool is used for cooking and cleaning. Wealthy Iranians, however, may live much as people in Europe or America live.

United Press International

Who are the Turkish people?

The Turkish people are largely descendants of people from Asia. Their language is similar to that spoken by some ancient peoples who lived in the Ural Mountains of Europe and Asia. Among the smaller groups of people living in Turkey are the Arabs and the Kurds. Almost all the people of Turkey follow the Islamic religion. Many of the people in the farm and city areas wear clothing similar to that worn in Europe or America.

For the past forty years, the government of Turkey has been working hard to improve this country. It is growing to be a modern country with laws much like those of European countries. Turkish women have equal rights with the men.

Most of the Turkish people make their living through farming or raising animals. The few who live in the cities are finding work in the nation's growing factories. On the farms, modern methods and machinery are replacing older farming customs.

Industry in the Middle East

So far, we have seen that most Middle-East peoples make their living through farming. We have not talked about the kind of life a farmer of the Middle East has. Is farming a good life? Are there any other important sources of income for the Middle East?

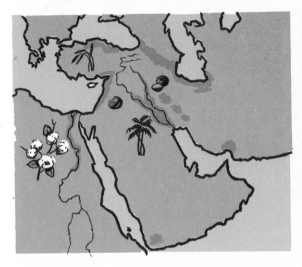

Do farmers make a good living?

The amount of suitable farmland in the Middle East is very small. Nevertheless, more than two-thirds of all the people are farmers. The farms are very small and each field within a farm is even smaller. The fields surround the villages where the people live. Usually every member of a family, men, women, and children must work in the fields.

'Round the World

Most families can grow enough only to feed themselves. Even so, they must pay taxes and usually part of their crops to a landlord who owns the land they farm. Giving part of their crops to a landlord means that most farm families do not get enough food to eat.

33

Landlord

Overseer

Fellahin

What is a farm village like?

An average Middle-East farm village has about fifty houses and about 250 people. The land the people farm stretches in a circle about two miles around the village. Each family farms a total of about eight acres. These acres are divided into several different fields located in different places around the village. The farmer and his family spend much time walking between the various fields during a working day.

The landlord, who lives far away in a city, owns the village, all the houses, the oxen used to work the fields, and all the seed that is used for planting. The landlord supplies all the tools needed. In return for all this, the farmers must pay him more than half the crops they harvest. The landlord seldom even sees his land or the people who work on it. He has an overseer, or kind of manager, who supervises the village. The overseer collects the rents and taxes and sends them to the landlord.

The only things the average villagers own are the clothes they wear and perhaps a few goats and sheep. Goats are very important in the Middle East because they can eat any kind of plant and they give milk. The farmers get milk and cheese from the goats, and wool and a little meat from the sheep.

What farming methods are used?

For the most part, farming in the Middle East is carried on in the same way and with the same kind of tools as in the days of the ancient Egyptians and Sumerians. Little progress has been made in changing to modern methods.

These workers are using a very old method for separating the grain from the chaff.

United Press International

Modern farm machinery costs a great deal of money. Middle East farmers have never had much money. In addition, the fields are so small that it would make little sense to use huge machinery. A tractor would not be very useful in a field so small that the farmer would have to stop and turn around every fifty feet.

Much of the machinery is made of wood and pulled by oxen or other animals. In the picture, a camel is used to pull the farmer's crude wooden plow over the ground.

Most farmlands in the Middle East could not be used without the help of irrigation. In many places, the irrigation methods the farmers use are as old and out-of-date as their other farming methods.

Wide World

How does farming in Israel differ from farming in other parts of the Middle East?

A farming village in Israel today is very different from the average village of other Middle-East countries. In Israel, there are many collective farms. A <u>collective farm</u>, called a <u>kibbutz</u> in Israel, is a farm on which all the people together own the land.

On a kibbutz, the Israeli people live together and work together.

They live in big apartment-like houses. They all eat together in a large dining room. These Israeli people are stopping to rest during their work of building houses.

The farmland is made up of large fields. Many people work at one time in the field. They can use large farm machinery because the fields are large.

Publix

Publix

A typical kibbutz has about 1,000 members. It has several thousand acres of farmland, about 1,000 of which are used to grow grains such as wheat and barley. About 200 acres are used to grow hay or other animal feed; about 100 are planted in fruit trees; and about 100 are used to grow vegetables. In addition, the kibbutz has its own livestock. There are no horses or mules, however, for the work is done with tractors and modern plows, harrows, harvesters, and other farm equipment.

The farm people of the new country of Israel have shown that, with hard work and planning, it is possible to develop prosperous farms in the poor lands of the Middle East.

What crops are grown?

Middle-East farmers, depending upon where they live, grow many different crops. The most important ones are the food crops. These are usually <u>cereals</u>, or grains such as wheat, barley, millet, rice, and corn.

In a few regions, crops are raised to be sold rather than for food. Such crops are called <u>cash crops</u>. The valuable long-fibered cotton grown in the Nile Valley of Egypt is an important cash crop.

About three-fourths of the world's dates are grown in and around the Tigris-Euphrates Valley of Iraq. Dates are the second important cash crop of the Middle East.

Some citrus fruits, such as oranges and lemons, are grown along the Mediterranean coast in Lebanon, Syria, and Israel. These are often shipped to Europe for sale.

Publix

Who are the nomadic herders?

The picture of farming in the Middle East would not be complete without mention of the nomads. A <u>nomad</u> is a person who does not have a permanent home. He wanders from place to place, taking all his belongings with him. He usually lives in a tent that he can fold and carry. He makes his living by raising animals, mostly sheep and goats.

Many of the nomads of the Middle East live in Iran. They spend the summer in the high mountain meadows of the Zagros Mountains. In the fall, they begin a long journey to the south central part of the country. Some of them travel as far as 350 miles. When spring comes, they start the trip back to the mountains.

Publix

All that they own they take with them, including their large flocks of sheep and goats. They do not own much, for they are very poor. The Bedouins are nomads that live in the deserts of Arabia. Food is scarce here. These people have been known to rob others for food.

39

What is manufactured in the Middle East?

Wide World

There are very few large factories in the Middle East. Most of the people who work in the cities make rugs, jewelry, pottery, hand tools, and the like. They make these by hand in small shops that employ only a few people. They are very skilled at their work, but they can produce only a few items, even over a long period of time.

The few factories that do exist in the Middle East are in Egypt, Turkey, and Israel. In Egypt, near Cairo, there are huge cotton mills where thousands of people work. These people tend the machines that produce cotton cloth from the cotton grown along the Nile River.

With the exception of its oil fields, the Middle East as a whole has few raw materials to use in manufacturing. There is little fuel to be used. These things make it hard for industries to grow.

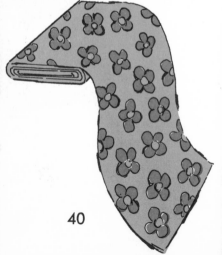

United Press International

40

Through the hard work of the Turkish government and people, there are now more than half a million people working in Turkish factories. They produce such things as shoes, clothing, tools, and even machinery that can be used to start new factories.

Wide World

Israel, though one of the smallest Middle-East countries, has more industry than the others. One reason for this is that many of the people of Israel have moved there from other countries. Most of these people were educated. They could easily learn the skills needed to work in industry. A second reason for Israel's industrial growth is that a great deal of money has been given by other countries to help Israel.

Today, Israel has many thriving industries. For the most part, the people make things that are small and require great skill to make. Examples would be watches, jewelry, needlework, and fine instruments like those used by doctors and scientists.

Wide World

The products shown in the pictures were all made by people working in their homes. Every item is handmade.

41

Where are the oil fields of the Middle East?

The Middle East is often considered one of the world's poorest regions. In one respect, however, parts of the Middle East are among the world's richest regions. These parts are the oil fields located in Iraq, Arabia, and Iran. One-fifth of all the oil now used in the world is drilled in these countries. Two-thirds of the world's known oil reserves, or oil still in the ground, are located in the Persian Gulf region of the Middle East. Unfortunately, there is no oil in other sections of the Middle East. The search for other oil reserves has been unsuccessful.

Who owns the Middle-East oil?

Oil was discovered in the Middle East in 1908. As might be expected in such a poor region of the world, the money to develop the oil industry was not available in Iraq, Iran, or Arabia. Oil companies from other countries of the world have invested money in the Middle East and developed the oil industry there.

Major Oil-Producing Countries of the World

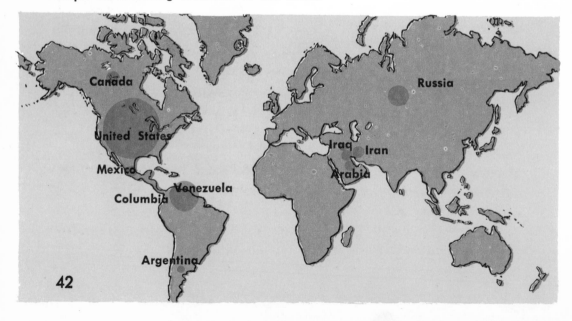

Kaufmann and Fabry

United States companies, in particular, have invested many millions of dollars in Middle-East oil. In Arabia, four American oil companies joined together to form <u>Aramco</u>, the Arabian-American Oil Company. This field is one of the largest oil fields in the world. Eight-hundred fifty Americans and 10,000 Arabians work there. Aramco Field looks a little like a town. There are homes, schools, stores, and churches for the American and Arabian workers. The picture shows oil storage tanks at Aramco.

In Iraq, Americans have joined with the French and British to form the Iraq Petroleum Company. The Qatar Petroleum Company is also owned by the British, the French, and the Americans. The Kuwait and Bahrain oil-producing areas are owned by British and American companies.

In Iran, however, the oil fields are owned by the government of Iran. American, Dutch, French, and British companies first developed these fields, but the government of Iran took them over in 1951. Iran cannot operate these oil fields without the help of engineers and trained specialists from the countries which first developed them. Now these original foreign owners operate the Iranian fields and share the profits with the government of that country.

What is done with Middle-East oil incomes?

Although foreign companies have invested millions of dollars to develop Middle-East oil fields, the foreign investors do not receive all the profits. To pay for the privilege of taking the oil, the oil companies turn over a large part of their profits to the governments of Iraq, Arabia, Kuwait, Bahrain, and Qatar. It must be remembered that these countries really own the oil, for it is under their land that the oil is found.

Each year the governments of the oil-producing countries receive many millions of oil dollars. Some of this money is being spent wisely to further education, irrigation projects, and public health. Yet, much remains to be done in these areas.

Where is Middle-East oil refined?

As it comes from the ground, oil is a thick, black liquid that is not of much use to anybody. It must be refined before it can be made into the gasolines, lubricating oils, and chemicals used all over the world. Chemical plants which do this refining are called <u>refineries</u>.

Refineries are expensive to build and operate. The oil-producing area has a few refineries: one is at Abadan, Iran, the largest in the world; and another is at Kirkuk in Iraq. Much of the oil is refined outside the Middle East.

Most of the oil is shipped by tanker through the Suez Canal to European refineries. The rest is pumped through six pipelines to refineries in Syria, Lebanon, and Israel. In this way, countries which have no oil themselves can share in the profits of the oil industry. Perhaps the money received from oil can help the Middle East to build other industries.

United Press International

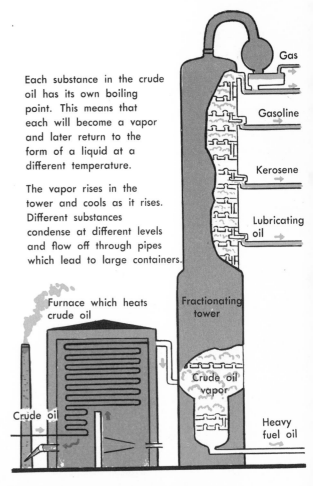

Each substance in the crude oil has its own boiling point. This means that each will become a vapor and later return to the form of a liquid at a different temperature.

The vapor rises in the tower and cools as it rises. Different substances condense at different levels and flow off through pipes which lead to large containers.

Gas

Gasoline

Kerosene

Lubricating oil

Fractionating tower

Furnace which heats crude oil

Crude oil vapor

Crude oil

Heavy fuel oil

JORDAN

QATAR

ISRAEL

KUWAIT

BAHREIN

TURKEY

SAUDI ARABIA

IRAQ

IRAN

OMAN

LEBANON

YEMEN

SYRIA

SOUTH ARABIA

Middle Eastern Governments

What types of governments are found in the Middle East?

First, let us define what is meant by <u>government</u>. Government is the political authority of a state or nation.

In the West, the usual form of government is democratic. That is, government by the people, as in the United States.

In the Soviet Union and China the form of government is <u>communistic</u>. That is, a system of total control by the Communist Party.

In the Middle East, however, many forms of government are found. They include: socialist, religious, republic, dictatorship, military rule, kingdoms, and sheikdoms.

Since many of the governments of the Middle East are varied, we will study the governments as they are found in Egypt, Iran, Iraq, Israel, Jordan, Lebanon, Saudi Arabia, Syria, and Turkey.

What kind of governments do Egypt and Iran have?

Egypt became an independent republic in 1953. The official name for Egypt is the Arab Republic of Egypt. Since 1953 Egypt has tried to unite several Arab countries into one state. First Egypt tried to set up the United Arab Republic. But this failed. Then it tried to set up the United Arab States. That effort also failed.

Egypt's constitution provides for a national and a <u>provincial</u>—local—government. The president is the executive head of the government. The provincial government is controlled by a council. Its members are chosen by the president.

The Council of the Nation holds the legislative power. But its members are chosen by the president. In effect, the government of Egypt is a <u>dictatorship</u>—complete control of the government—by the president.

Egyptian law also requires men over the age of 18 to serve in the armed forces. Men who have not had a high-school education serve three years. High-school graduates serve only 18 months.

In Iran, the constitution of 1906 set up a <u>constitutional monarchy</u>—government in which the king's power is limited. The <u>Shah</u>—King—of Iran is the head of state. But the prime minister is the political leader of the nation as well as the executive head of government.

The shah's oldest son succeeds to the throne. If the shah has no son, he chooses a male heir to rule. The choice, however, is approved by parliament.

There are two houses of parliament, the Senate and the <u>Majlis</u>—National Assembly. The voters elect thirty senators and the shah chooses thirty senators. By law, half the senators come from the capital city of Tehran. The prime minister is chosen by the shah. But to remain in office, the prime minister must maintain the support of parliament.

Iran has no political parties. Men and women over the age of 21, who can read and write, may vote.

Iranian law also requires men between the ages of 18 and 28 to serve in the armed forces for two years.

What kind of government does Israel have?

British control over Palestine ended in 1948. On May 14, of that year, Palestine declared its independence and became the Republic of Israel.

The president is the head of state. He chooses one of the members of the <u>Knesset</u>—Parliament—to serve as prime minister. The prime minister is the political leader of the nation as well as the executive head of the government.

The Knesset holds the legislative power. Its 120 members are elected for four-year terms. The election is held under a system known as proportional representation. That is, the citizens elect political parties, not individuals as in the United States. The Israeli system is similar to that used in Italy and France.

Israeli law is based on British law, Turkish law, and the Israeli constitution.

Wide World

Associated Press

What kind of governments do Jordan, Syria, Iraq, and Lebanon have?

In Jordan, the constitution of 1952 set up a constitutional monarchy. The king is the head of state. But the prime minister is the political leader of the nation as well as the executive head of government.

The National Assembly holds the legislative power. It has two houses, the Council of Notables and the Council of Representatives. The king chooses the members of the Council of Notables for four-year terms. The voters elect the members of the Council of Representatives. These members also serve four-year terms. The king has the power to veto laws passed by the National Assembly, but the assembly can override his veto.

The Court of Appeal is the nation's highest court. But the <u>Sharia</u>—Moslem religious courts—handle religious questions of law.

There are several political parties in Jordan. Men over the age of 18 may vote.

Jordan's volunteer army assists the nation's police.

Syria became an independent republic in 1941. Soon after, the army tried to control the government. For years, Syria underwent many revolts, new constitutions, and dictators. Some stability was achieved when Syria became part of the United Arab Republic. But in 1961, the Syrians revolted again. Then, Syrian army officers set up a military government in 1962. At present, the army enforces military rule in Syria.

In Iraq, a six-man junta—military leaders—took control of the Iraqi government in 1963. Iraq is under a military dictatorship. The junta president is Iraq's head of state. In this nation, the army also enforces the rule of the military junta.

For Lebanon, France helped form a republican government in 1926. The Lebanese constitution provides for a system of government by religious groups. This system is known as confessional representation. That is, each religious group elects representatives in proportion to its size.

Confessional representation was thought necessary because about half of the Lebanese are Christians, the other half are Moslems. The Christian population is divided into many groups. The largest is the Maronite Christians. The Moslems are divided into Sunni and Shiites.

Under Lebanese law, the president of Lebanon is always a Christian. The prime minister, always a Sunni Moslem, is the executive head of the government. The head of the parliament is always a Shiite Moslem.

Because the Lebanese government is chosen on the basis of religion, there are no political parties. By law, those citizens who are qualified are required to vote.

What kind of governments do Saudi Arabia and Turkey have?

Early in the 1900's, Abdul Aziz Ibn Saud conquered Nejd and Hejaz with his army. Saud proclaimed himself king, and in 1932 he changed the country's name to Saudi Arabia.

Saudi Arabia is a monarchy. The king is an absolute ruler. That is, he has complete control of the government and his word is law. The king is also the <u>Imam</u>—religious leader—of Saudi Arabia.

The king's eldest son, or brother, is usually the prime minister. The king chooses members of a cabinet to help him in matters of state. He also chooses the members of the Consultative Assembly. This assembly can pass laws. However, the laws must be approved by the king. The assembly has no set number of members but it usually includes the cabinet and other high officials.

Saudi Arabia is divided into the viceroyalties of Hejaz and Nejd. They are ruled by viceroys who usually are sons of the king.

Saudi Arabia has a small volunteer army and air force.

Turkey became an independent republic in 1923. It was the first Moslem nation to separate religion from affairs of state. Turkey is also the only Arab nation whose territory extends into Europe. European Turkey is separated from the Middle East by the Bosporus. The Bosporus is the only passage between the Black Sea and the Mediterranean.

In 1961, a new constitution formed the Second Republic. The Grand National Assembly holds the legislative power. It also elects the President of Turkey for seven years.

The Grand National Assembly has two houses, the National Assembly and the Senate. The Senate has 150 members elected by the voters for six-year terms. But fifteen of them are chosen by the president. The president also chooses a prime minister with the approval of the assembly. The voters elect 450 members to the National Assembly for a four-year term of office.

Wide World

Turkey is divided into 67 vilayets—provinces. Each vilayet is controlled by a vali—governor—who is appointed by the president of Turkey.

Until 1945, Turkey had one political party. It was the government's party. Since then, several political parties have been allowed in the Turkish elections. By law, those citizens who are qualified are allowed to vote.

Turkish law requires men to serve in the armed forces for two years. Turkey has one of the largest armed forces in the Middle East. Since 1952, Turkey has been a member of NATO (North Atlantic Treaty Organization).

What is a sheikdom?

A sheik is an Arabic title of respect. It is held by the leaders of religious groups, chiefs of tribes, and headmen of villages.

The sheik holds the executive power of government. Some sheiks lead their followers and control the affairs of the tribe in the manner of a king. Other sheiks have little influence. Thus, the power of a sheik depends on his will.

Kuwait and Qatar are independent sheikdoms under British protection.

Wide World

What kind of governments do Oman, United Arab Emirates, Aden, and Yemen have?

The full name of Oman is the Sultanate of Masqat and Oman. It is an independent *sultanate*—ruled by a sultan or king.

The United Arab Emirates is a union of seven sheikdoms. The sheikdoms are Abu Dhabi, Dibai, Sharja and Kalba, Ajman, Fujaira, Umm al Qaywayn, and Ras al Khymah.

The United Arab Emirates union started with the truces, or agreements, made between the sheikdoms and the British government. In these truces, the sheikdoms agreed to deal only with Great Britain.

Aden is also called Yemen (Aden) to distinguish it from Yemen (Sana), its next door neighbor. Aden is a republic governed by an executive committee, called the National Front. Yemen (Aden) is divided into six parts, each run by a governor.

Since 1974 Yemen (Sana) has been governed by a group of five army officers.

Wide World

57

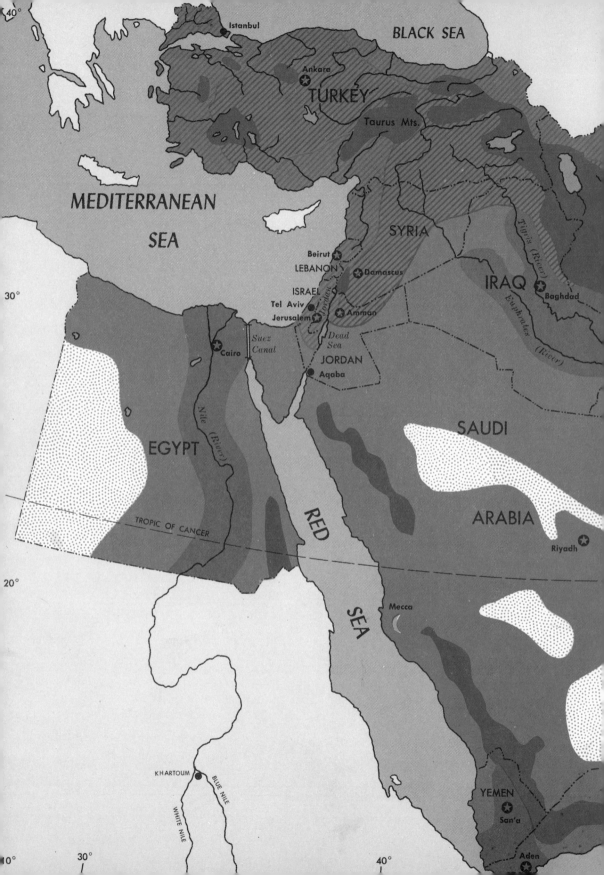

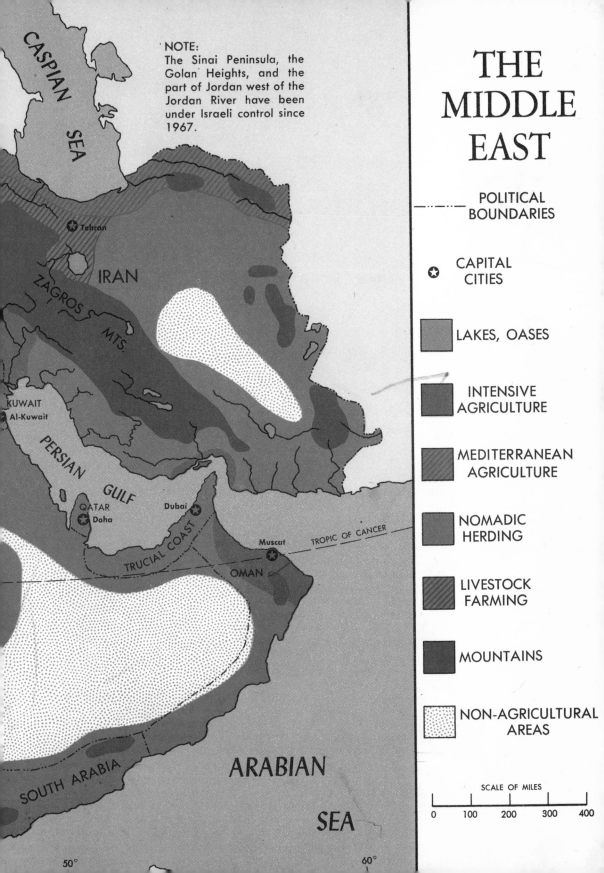

THE MIDDLE EAST

CASPIAN SEA

NOTE:
The Sinai Peninsula, the
Golan Heights, and the
part of Jordan west of the
Jordan River have been
under Israeli control since
1967.

Tehran

IRAN

ZAGROS MTS.

KUWAIT
Al-Kuwait

PERSIAN GULF

QATAR
Doha

Dubai

TRUCIAL COAST

Muscat

TROPIC OF CANCER

OMAN

SOUTH ARABIA

ARABIAN

SEA

50°   60°

POLITICAL
BOUNDARIES

CAPITAL
CITIES

LAKES, OASES

INTENSIVE
AGRICULTURE

MEDITERRANEAN
AGRICULTURE

NOMADIC
HERDING

LIVESTOCK
FARMING

MOUNTAINS

NON-AGRICULTURAL
AREAS

SCALE OF MILES

0   100   200   300   400

An Area of Problems

The people of the Middle East face many problems: over-crowded land, lack of water, poverty, disease, and lack of education. Each one of these problems helps to cause the other four—all of the problems are related.

What is the land problem in the Middle East?

The Middle East covers a large land area. Most of the land, however, is unused because it is too dry for farming. Much of the land is desert where it seldom ever rains.

The people live crowded together in the few areas where there is enough water for farming. The map shows the population density, or the number of people living in the area shown.

POPULATION DENSITY

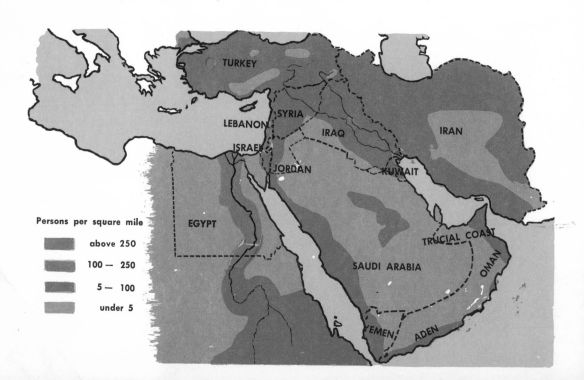

Persons per square mile

above 250

100 — 250

5 — 100

under 5

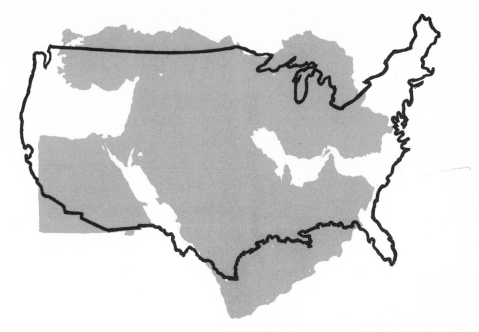

Most of the people live in the Nile Valley, the Tigris-Euphrates Valley, and along the seacoasts. Since all of Egypt outside the Nile Valley is desert, almost all the Egyptian people live in the Nile Valley. As many as twenty-five hundred persons live on each square mile of the fertile Nile Valley. By comparison, the most crowded state of the United States, Rhode Island, has 811 persons per square mile. Very few of these people, however, have to make their living from farming.

If the population of the Nile Valley were spread throughout the whole country of Egypt, the density would be only about ninety-seven persons per square mile. This is only a bit more than the United States, where the density is sixty persons per square mile. as a national average.

The area of the Middle East is almost as great as that of the United States. Less people live in the Middle East than in the United States. The serious over-crowding comes from the fact that people all try to live in the few areas where farming is possible.

'Round the World

How does present irrigation help the land problem?

As long as most of the people make their living by farming, they cannot use the areas where little rain falls unless water can be brought to the land by irrigation. Irrigation has been used in the Tigris-Euphrates Valley and in the Nile Valley for centuries. The methods used today are not much improved from the irrigation methods used by ancient peoples. Using these methods, the Middle East peoples cannot hope to irrigate nearly as much land as is needed.

United Press International

'Round the World

The men in the pictures above are each turning a type of hand pump. The picture on the right shows paddle-wheel pumps like those first used by the ancient Egyptians.

What are the living conditions of the people?

The Middle East is one of the poorest regions of the world. It is poor in resources, in industry, water, and farmlands. We would expect the people to be very poor, since most of them depend upon farming to make a living.

Because of the over-crowding, each family must live on the income from only a few acres of land. The farmers usually do not own the land they work. They are <u>tenant farmers</u>, which means they rent the land from landowners. There are many tenant farmers and few landowners. These landowners usually hold a great deal of land. Most of them live in the cities.

Wide World

Rents are very high. Tenants sometimes pay as much as three-fifths of their crop in the form of rent. This leaves the farmer only two-fifths of his small crop to use in feeding and clothing his family.

Many farm families do not get enough to eat, nor do they have proper clothes to wear. More than two-thirds of the people of the Middle East are farmers and most of them live in extreme poverty and need.

The little girl in the picture is holding a bottle of milk given to her by a United Nations organization.

Those who live in towns and cities are no better off. Wages are very low in the few industries that have been set up. There are more men looking for work than there are jobs. There are not enough houses to give all the people shelter.

It would be safe to say that ninety percent of the people in this large and important region of the world go to bed hungry every night. They don't starve, but they never have enough food.

How does poverty affect health conditions?

Disease goes along with poverty, or being poor and needy. When people are too poor to eat properly, they are also too poor to afford decent housing and clean living conditions. Such conditions cause much sickness in the Middle East.

The average farm village has no underground sewage systems. Sewage runs into open ditches, poisoning the air and water supply. Many disease germs grow in the sewage.

Although new housing projects have been undertaken in the cities, many poor people still live in dirty, unhealthful mud huts.

Wide World

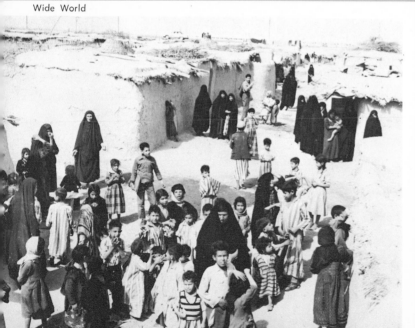

These people live in the poor section of the ancient city of Baghdad. Other parts of this city have beautiful buildings and wide, paved streets. The wealthy people live there.

Everywhere in Middle-East villages and cities there are millions of flies. They breed in filth and spread disease. <u>Dysentery</u>, a disease of the intestinal tract, is very common throughout the area. It is carried by flies and impure drink-

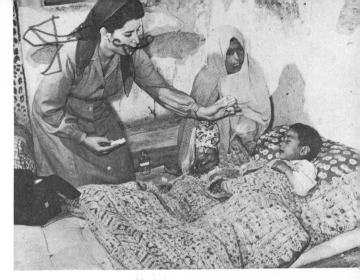

ing water. Malaria, a serious disease carried by certain mosquitoes, is another common disease of the Middle East.

In a few areas, the people had to find new homes because the malaria germs were so plentiful. Even in fertile areas, people have been forced to move because of disease.

Diseases that cause blindness and crippling are common in the Middle East. Most of these sicknesses could be controlled by sanitation and medicines that are plentiful in other parts of the world today.

Ringworm and other skin diseases are spread among people who know nothing of sanitary measures and who often have little water and no soap.

The death rate is very high, particularly among children. Every year many thousands of babies and young children die of dysentery, malaria, and other diseases. In some farm areas, half of the babies die before they are one year old.

Yet, millions of people do live on. Their bodies develop the ability to throw off disease germs or to live in spite of the disease. Many persons spend their entire lives in poor health.

What educational opportunities do the people have?

Where poverty and disease are common, there is usually little educational opportunity. In a group of thirty-six villages in Iran, there are only three schools. This is a common situation in the Middle East. In large areas, there are no schools at all. When schools do exist, they usually have only three or four grades. In such schools, children are lucky if they learn to read or write.

The picture on page 67 shows a common sight throughout the Middle East. The man with the writing materials is a letter-writer. One of the other men, who cannot read or write, is paying the letter-writer to do some writing for him. These letter-writers are found mostly in the cities.

Without education, the people can hardly be expected to solve the difficult problems of land use, irrigation, sanitation, and disease. When most of the children do not even learn to read and write, it is impossible to train the scientists, doctors, and engineers that are needed. Without doctors and scientists, the problems of disease cannot be overcome. Without engineers and skilled workers, the Middle East must remain a land of little industry.

Wide World

Lawyers, writers, and statesmen could change the lives of the people. Because the people are uneducated, the few more fortunate people of their country often do not even consider the needs of their poor countrymen. Trained leaders could help the poor people to get fairer treatment.

What other problems do the Middle-East people face?

Lack of transportation is one reason it has been hard for industry to grow in the Middle East. Good roads and railroads are needed to bring raw materials to the factories. Roads are needed to carry finished products to markets and seaports. The Middle East does not have such roads. Most of the roads that do exist are narrow and unpaved. There are very few railroads.

Travel and transportation today are much as they were centuries ago. In Arabia, camels are still used to bring goods to market. The man on the donkey is riding his animal to Jerusalem over a road that is hundreds of years old. He will get food and supplies to take back to his home.

On the whole, there is little travel in the Middle East. The few wealthy people buy cars from foreign countries. The poor people walk, ride camels or donkeys, or ride in carts pulled by oxen.

Is there cooperation among Middle-East countries?

Friendship among the countries of the Middle East would make the solving of their problems easier. Yet, little friendship exists. The new state of Israel has not been accepted by the Arab countries. As soon as it became independent, the armies of four Arab countries attacked it. The United Nations ended the fighting in 1949. After that, thousands of Arabs living in Israel left to live in Arab countries. Since 1949, these people have been living in refugee camps in Jordan and Egypt. The picture shows mothers and children at the feeding center in one of these camps.

Wide World

Even among the Arab countries, there are differences which make cooperation difficult. Egypt and Syria tried to work together when they formed the United Arab Republic in 1958. This experiment ended in 1961. An important group of people in Syria decided that the plan was not helping Syria.

Toward the Future

In the last chapter, we learned of the many problems faced by the people of the Middle East. In this chapter, we shall discuss ways in which these problems could be solved. We shall consider some of the steps that the countries of this area could take to help themselves. We shall also talk about ways in which the richer countries of the world could help the Middle-East people.

Wide World

How could irrigation help?

The overcrowded living conditions in the fertile regions could be changed through the building of large modern irrigation systems. Barren areas could be watered to make new farmlands. Many of the people could move to new farms.

The picture shows King Hussein of Jordan at the opening of a modern irrigation canal.

Steps are being taken in several areas to build new irrigation works. Egypt has built a new dam at Aswan. This dam stores more water than the old one. It makes possible many more miles of irrigation ditches along the Nile.

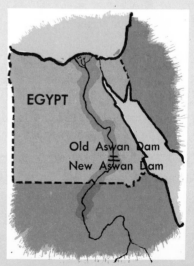

EGYPT

Old Aswan Dam
New Aswan Dam

The picture shows the huge dam at Aswan. The dam caused some of the ancient buildings and statues located nearby to be completely covered by water all year round.

The Aswan Dam is only part of a large plan the Egyptian government has for trying to help some of the poor farmers of this country. The picture shows a village that has been built in the western desert region of Egypt. The land around the village can now be farmed because of the new irrigation projects.

Egypt hopes to build many villages like this one on new lands made fertile through irrigation. This Egyptian farmer and his family find their new home much different from their old mud hut.

At present, only certain farm families are chosen to be moved to the new lands and new villages. If the plan is successful, however, many Egyptian farmers may be living in similar villages.

Iraq, too, is trying to do something about building irrigation systems. Iraq is paid many millions of dollars each year for her oil. Some of this money is placed in a fund for the Development Plan the government has set up for this country. Under this Development Plan, Iraq hopes to use the waters of the Tigris and the Euphrates Rivers to bring water to new farms in the valley.

United Press International

At Dokan, Iraq, a huge dam is being built for use in irrigation and flood control in this area. Later, Iraq hopes to use the dam to provide electric power. The size of this tunnel gives an idea of what a huge building project this dam is.

Iraq is making progress, but it is very slow. Such projects cost a great deal of money. To be really successful they must have the cooperation of other countries to allow other dams to be built.

The Tigris and Euphrates both rise in the mountains of Turkey. They flow for some distance through Syria. Dams must be built in these two countries also to store water for year-round use. As yet, these dams are not being built.

Israel has suggested plans for using the Jordan River for irrigation in both countries. Jordan refuses to cooperate.

72

Israel has worked to build irrigation systems throughout the country. These huge pipes are being made at an Israeli manufacturing plant near Tel Aviv. They will be used in the irrigation of the barren Negev area in Israel. The pipes are made after an American design.

Publix

Many areas are being helped by new irrigation. Yet, until the needed dams are built on the Tigris, Euphrates, and Jordan rivers, many people will go on living on crowded farmlands.

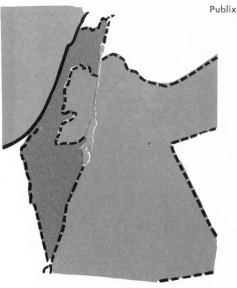

How could water distillation help?

The lands of the Middle East are surrounded by seas: the Mediterranean, the Red, the Black, the Caspian, and the Persian Gulf. It would seem that these bodies of water could supply Middle-East countries with water. Sea water, however, is salty. It cannot be used for drinking or for irrigation until the salt has been removed.

Salt can be removed from sea water through <u>distillation</u>. In this process, the salt water is heated until steam rises from it. When the steam cools and changes back to water, the water is pure.

Some distillation is done in the Middle East, but only in small amounts. The man in the picture is taking water distilled from the Red Sea into the city of Jidda. During the day, he will sell water from the tank cart to people living in the city.

Distillation of large amounts of water is a very costly process. First, huge plants must be built where millions of gallons of water can be boiled. Secondly, great amounts of fuels such as gas, oil, or coal must be burned to heat the water.

It is possible that some day the Middle East may realize the hope of distilling sea water. Distillation plants powered by atomic energy would not be too expensive for the people to operate. It would cost a great deal to build such plants, much more than the peoples of the Middle East could afford. They would need help from the richer countries of the world. Once built, however, they could operate for many years at low cost. They could supply amounts of pure water which could be piped from the seacoasts to dry areas where water is so badly needed.

How can public health be improved?

Control of the disease problem must begin with the control of sewage and insects. This could be done by setting up public health projects, as was done in the villages of Kaber and Babbila in Syria. In these two villages, little disease exists today.

Both now have closed sewers and sewage is chemically treated to kill disease germs. Drinking water comes from wells deep in the earth. Water from each well is tested regularly to make sure it is free from germs. The villages are sprayed regularly with DDT, so there are very few flies to carry diseases.

What has been done in Kaber and Babbila was done under the leadership of the Near East Foundation, an American organization with private funds.

In the top picture, Arab children are being vaccinated by Israeli doctors. These children are returning to their homes in Israel after the Jordan-Israeli trouble in the late forties.

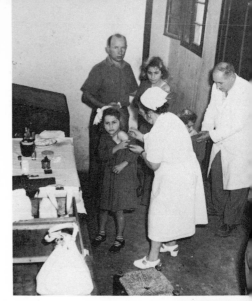

Wide World

Wide World

In the second picture, the men are carrying DDT sprayers on their backs. They will spray the members of this mountain family and many others in order to destroy malaria-carrying mosquitoes. This picture was taken in Iraq, where the government is taking steps to rid the country of malaria.

In some areas, new housing is improving health conditions. The old, dirty buildings in the upper picture were once the homes of people in Beersheba, Israel. Today, they have been replaced by the clean, modern apartment buildings shown in the lower picture. The new buildings are plain and not very expensive, but they give the people a healthier place to live.

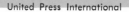

How could the system of land ownership be changed?

As we have seen before, most of the people of the Middle East are poor tenant farmers. If conditions stay the same in these countries, the tenant farmers will live on in poverty.

In some areas, where farmers have been allowed to own the land themselves, great changes have taken place. The farmers keep more of the farm income for themselves, in place of paying heavy taxes to landlords. The farmers feel like working harder and taking pride in what they are doing. They know they will be able to keep what they earn.

The village of Siblene, in Lebanon, was once just like any other Middle-East farming village. It was owned by a landlord and worked by poor tenant farmers. The landlord of Siblene, however, was wiser and more generous than most landlords. He decided to sell the houses and the land to the farmers at a very low price. He gave them several years to pay him the money. When the landlord did this, it seemed that a miracle took place.

Siblene changed almost overnight. Now that they were the owners, the people took an interest in their houses, their farms, and the village. They worked much harder than they had before. The mud houses were cleaned and even painted; curtains hung at the windows; flowers or shrubs were planted. New groves of fruit and olive trees were planted. Even a school was built in this village that had never had one before.

Siblene shows what could happen in other places. Unfortunately, not all the landlords are like the former landlord of Siblene. Perhaps the land could be bought from the landlords and then resold to the farmers at low prices. Some of the countries might use their oil incomes to buy the land from landlords. Still more money would be needed, however, if this plan were put into use.

How can education help the people?

Looking at the many problems of the Middle East, one might wonder how such conditions could exist in the twentieth century. One might ask why the people themselves have not done something long before now to improve their difficult lives. The answer is that few people of this area even know that there is a better way to live. Those few people who have gone to school barely learned to read and write. They learned nothing of living standards in other parts of the world.

Publix

Through education the people could be made to realize that dirt and flies cause sickness. They could learn new ways of farming to increase the size of their crops. They could learn skills that would help them to set up new industries.

Of course, education calls for schools. Thousands of school buildings need to be built. They need not be as large or as expensive as those in Europe or America. Yet, they will cost money, more money than the Middle East has. Of course, teachers will be needed for the schools, and it will take still more money to train teachers. Other countries have already helped to build schools and train teachers. Yet, more will be needed before these people can be educated to help themselves and their children.

The Jewish people have placed great importance on education in the rebuilding of Israel. Above is shown one of the new, modern buildings of the Institute for Jewish Studies at Givath Ram.

One way to obtain schools and to raise the standard of education may be to speed the changes in land ownership. As the land-owning farmers become more interested in their own and their children's lives, they will become more willing to pay taxes to build schools.

The Middle East
and the Free World

The world as a whole owes much to the Middle East for its early contributions to civilization. This was one of the major world areas in which civilization began and spread to other parts of the world. Three of the world's great religions, Judaism, Christianity, and Islam, were born there. Almost all the major countries of the Free World today are Christian nations. The task of these nations is to encourage and support government and private efforts to improve the living conditions of the people of the Middle East.

Wide World

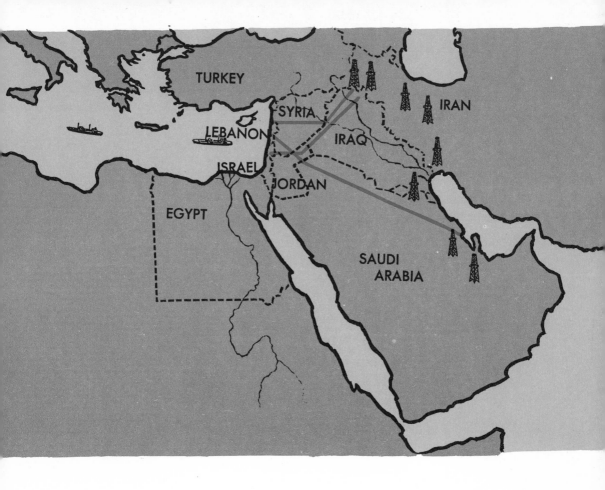

How is the future of the Middle East linked with the future of the Free World?

The oil in the Persian Gulf area of the Middle East is of great importance to the whole world. Modern industrial nations could not survive without the products of oil. In recent years, the United States alone has been producing about half the oil used throughout the world. This may mean that the United States will use so much of its own oil that it will someday have to depend upon oil from the Persian Gulf area. The Middle East is already supplying a large share of the oil used in Great Britain and Europe. This is an important reason why the countries of the Middle East must remain a part of the Free World.

81

How does Communism threaten the Middle East?

The Soviet Union would like to gain control of these countries and their oil. This would bring another large area under the influence of the Communist Party. Russia is not in danger of using up her own oil, but if she could control the oil of the Middle East, her influence over the industrial nations of the Free World would be greater than it is.

We know living conditions in the Middle East are poor. When people live this way, they are often ready to listen to the promises of the Communists. The Communists tell them that they will have enough to eat and be better off
if they join the Communist nations
of the world.

Wide World

Poor and uneducated people often have no way of knowing that the promises of the Communists are false promises. They do not know that many of the people of Communist countries live no better than they themselves do.

The nations of the free world must work to keep the Middle East from falling into the hands of the Communists. This calls for an understanding of the problems and well-designed plans for solving them. We have seen what some of these plans must include and how some of them have already been put into action. Yet, much remains to be done in the land of the Middle East.

Wide World

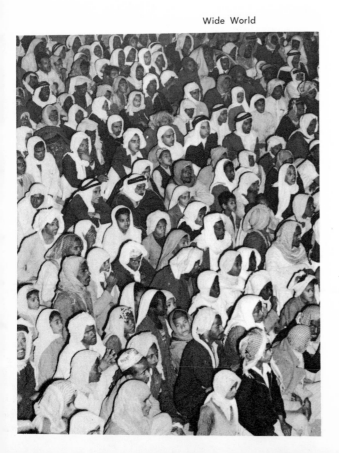

Official Languages of the Middle East

Nation	Language
Egypt	Arabic
Iran	Persian
Iraq	Arabic
Israel	Arabic and Hebrew
Jordan	Arabic
Kuwait	Arabic
Lebanon	Arabic
Oman	Arabic
Qatar	Arabic
Saudi Arabia	Arabic
Aden	Arabic
Syria	Arabic
United Arab Emirates	Arabic
Turkey	Turkish
Yemen	Arabic

What links the people of the Middle East together?

Although English and French are widely spoken by many Arabs, the first link in Middle Eastern unity is Arabic.

Arabic is the dominant language of the people of the Middle East. It is the official language of every Middle Eastern nation except for Turkey and Iran.

Another link is Islam. Mohammed helped unite the Arab tribes through the Islam religion.

The last link is the Arab's common wish to destroy Jewish dominance in Israel. Most Arabs want Palestinian refugees to return to their homes and help lead the state of Israel.

The Arabs and Israelis fought four wars: in 1948, 1955, 1967, and 1973. Hatred grew in the area.

Language, religion, and beliefs link the Middle East together. But the links that help hold the Arabs together also serve to keep them apart.

For example, political differences between Arab nations have led to war. The civil war in Yemen was also a war between Egypt and Saudi Arabia. The efforts of Egypt to create a United Arab Republic have ended in failure.

The political situation in the Middle East is very tense. The United States and other members of the United Nations fear that a nuclear war might erupt in the Middle East.

Lookout Mountain Laboratory, USAF

Religious differences also exist. Many Moslems belong to different Islamic religious groups. Sometimes their religious differences also led to war.

The Arabs are also divided in the manner in which they live—city, village, and nomadic.

Industrialization has changed the cities. Most of the industrial development has taken place in Egypt, Turkey, Iran, Iraq, Lebanon, and Syria with Israel being the most industrialized nation in the Middle East.

But the nomadic and village way of living and fashion of dress have changed little since the days of Mohammed.

Arabic-American Oil Company

Since World War II, social, economic, cultural, and political revolutions have brought many changes to the Middle East.

The people have demanded land reform, more education, improved sanitation and health facilities, and rapid industrialization.

Financial and technical help from the United States, the Soviet Union, and the United Nations have helped solve some of these problems. Were all Middle Eastern problems solved, Arab unity would remain skin deep. For beneath the surface, ancient tribal differences have been swept up by a new spirit of Arab nationalism which further divides the people of the Middle East.

How are the people of the Middle East citizens of the World?

The Middle East is a world center of trade. For centuries, the Middle East has been a trade route between the three continents of Europe, Africa, and Asia. Today, a fourth and fifth continent have been added—North and South America.

The discovery of oil in the Middle East has made this area more important. Oil is what helps turn the wheels of the industrialized nations. Thus, what happens in the Middle East is important to the industries of such nations as the Soviet Union and the United States.

But trade also carries ideas as well as goods. Throughout history, the Middle Eastern traders carried their religion, language, and literature from country to country.

Also from the Middle East come two of the most influential books in human history—the Bible and the Koran.

Judaism, Christianity, and Islamism were born in the deserts of the Middle East. Although each religion is different, each has been influenced by the other.

Both Judaism and Christianity use the Bible. In Judaism, the first five books of the Old Testament are known as the Torah. While, in Christianity, one usually thinks of the Gospels of the New Testament.

Whatever one may think of Judaism, Christianity, and Islamism their influence in the development of western and eastern cultures has been of great importance.

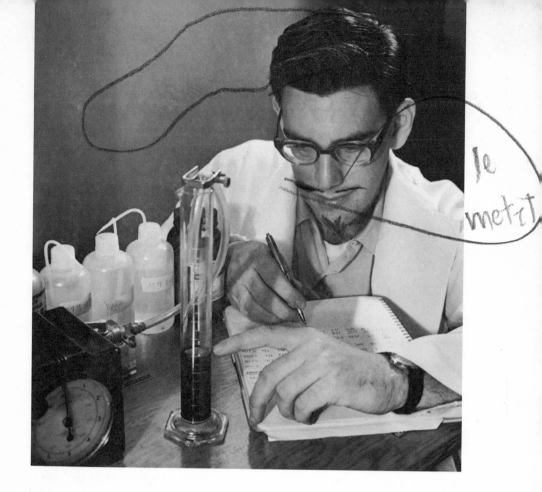

Here are ten symbols: 0, 1, 2, 3, 4, 5, 6, 7, 8, 9. You commonly use them. They are known as Arabic numerals. They are considered by mathematicians as one of the world's greatest inventions.

The greatness of Arabic numerals is found in two ideas—place value and the use of <u>zero</u>. Place value is the numerical quantity shown by position, as in 857. Zero is the number that does not change any number to which it is added. With these two ideas it is easy to write any number and to work out any mathematical problem.

Not so great? Try to show one thousand five without using zero. For more fun, try to represent five hundred three without using place value and zero.

90

Arabic is one of the important languages of the world.

It is an Afro-Asiatic language which includes Hebrew, Aramaic, and Ethiopic. Also spoken in the Middle East are Turkish and Persian.

On the following page is a chart. It gives a small sample of the Middle East influence in the English language.

English Words Borrowed from the Middle East

English	Arabic	Persian	Turkish	Hebrew
alfalfa	al-fasfasah			
algebra	al-jabr			
bazaar		bazar		
calendar		kalandar		
camel				gamal
caravan		karwan		
coffee	qahwah			
cotton	qutn			
gazelle	ghazal			
giraffe	zirafah			
harem	harim			
jar	jarrah			
lime	lim			
lute	al'ud			
magic		mogush		
peach		persicus		
safari	safariy			
sherbert	sharbah	sharbat	serbet	
sofa	suffah			
sugar	sukkar			
tulip			tulbend	
zero	sifr			

United Nations

What Middle Eastern nations belong to the United Nations?

The United Nations is an organization of nations who have joined together to maintain world peace.

With the exception of Kuwait who became a member in 1963, Egypt, Iran, Iraq, Israel, Lebanon, Saudi Arabia, Syria, Turkey, and Yemen joined the United Nations soon after the end of World War II.

Although many differences exist between the nations of the Middle East and the nations of other parts of the world, the fact that many nations of the world have joined the United Nations means they share in its goal.

93

Summary of Basic Concepts

This book has shown us how the Middle East was once a great center of civilization. We have seen how wars and invasions destroyed this civilization. For many years, the poor people of the Middle East lived in poverty and disease, almost forgotten by the more fortunate people of their own countries and by the rest of the world. Today, however, the world is taking a new interest in the Middle East. Perhaps even more important, the people of the Middle East are beginning to take a new interest in themselves and their lives.

The Middle East is an area of mixed population.
Pages: 23-26, 31-32, 39, 84-86

The countries discussed in this book usually agree on matters that concern this area as against the rest of the world. For this reason, the Middle East is often thought of as an "Arab region." All of the inhabitants of this region are not Arabs, however, for there are several different language and national groups spread throughout the countries. We have seen that the Arabs, those Moslems who speak the Arabic language, have especially strong feelings for their own group and wish to keep the Middle East mainly an Arab region. These strong feelings sometimes lead to trouble.

The Middle East is an area poor in industry.
Pages: 33-35, 39-40, 60-61, 63, 67-68

The Nile River Valley and the Tigris-Euphrates River Valley are among the world's richest farming areas. Aside from these two areas, the Middle East has very little natural farmland. Yet, almost eighty percent of the entire Middle-East population depends upon farming to make a living. Using crude methods of irrigation, plowing, planting, and the like, the farmers live crowded together in the small areas where their crops will grow. In many cases, they grow barely enough to keep themselves and their families alive.

Manufacturing is very limited in most countries. Outside of the cotton mills of Egypt, few factories have been built in Middle-East countries. Oil is the only natural resource that the Middle East has in any quantity. Only in recent years have the people been helped by the rich oil deposits.

The Middle East is an area of change.
Pages: 36-37, 41, 47-53, 70-73, 76-77, 89

In recent years, and especially since World War II, many of the poor countries of the world have begun to build up their industries and to set up more democratic forms of government. Changes like these have been taking place in the Middle East, too. Some of the countries are trying to help the poor farmers to get more land and better living conditions. Other countries are building factories and modern buildings in their cities. In some areas, much of the wealth that has been held by only a few people in the past is now being divided among the poor people. Public health projects are being set up to do away with dirt and disease.

The Middle East is an area important to the Free World.
Pages: 42-43, 80-82, 88, 93

Since the Middle East is an area of change, it is sometimes an area of trouble also. Change sometimes causes disagreement and even fighting. It is important to the Free World that the people of these countries make the changes they want in a peaceable way. Even small fights in the world today could lead to large fights or even war.

Because the people of the Middle East are ready for change, they could be willing to listen to anyone who promises to help them. The Communists know this. It is important that the Free World not allow the Communists to mislead the Middle-East peoples.

Since the discovery of oil in the Middle East, people from many nations of the Free World have helped the poor countries to build up oil industries. The oil industries are important to both the Middle-East countries and the Free World.

Glossary

The words shown below are underlined and defined in the text. The numbers indicate the pages on which the words first appear.

Aramco (ă răm′cō) 43 — four American oil companies investing in oil fields in Arabia, the Arabian-American Oil Company.

cash crop 38 — crops raised to be sold rather than for food.

cereals 38 — grains such as wheat, barley, millet, rice, and corn.

climate 11 — the average weather conditions of a certain region over a period of years.

collective farm 36 — a farm on which all the people together own the land.

continent 6 — one of the seven largest bodies of land into which the earth is divided.

Crusades 24 — wars the European Christians fought with the Turks.

cuneiform (kū′nē′ĭ fôrm) 19 — a kind of wedge-shaped letter that stands for a word or part of a word.

desert 10 — very dry, mostly sandy areas where almost no plants can live.

distillation (dĭs′tĭ lā′shŭn) 59 — process by which salt water is heated until steam rises from it; the steam then cools and changes back to pure water.

dysentery (dĭs′ĕn tĕr′ĭ) 51 — a disease of the intestinal tract.

fellahin (fĕl′a̍ hēn′) 29 — Arab farmers.

hieroglyphics (hī′ĕr ô glĭ′fĭx) 15 — Egyptian picture writing.

irrigation (ĭr′ĭ gā′shŭn) 15 — a method of bringing water to dry lands.

kibbutz (kĭb′ŭts) 36 — a farm in Israel on which all the people together own the land.

Moslems (mōz′lĕmz) 26 — followers of the Islamic religion.

nomad (nō′măd) 39 — a wanderer, without a permanent home.

oil reserves 42 — oil still in the ground.

papyrus (pa̍ pī′rŭs) 15 — a kind of paper made from seeds growing along the Nile.

plateau (pla̍ tō′) 10 — high, mostly flat land areas.

population density 46 — the number of people living in a specified area.

poverty 50 — the state of being poor or needy.

pyramid (pĭr′a̍ mĭd) 15 — huge pointed four-sided monuments of stone used by Egyptians for burial of royalty.

refineries 45 — Chemical plants which remove impurities from oil.

semi-arid (sĕm′ĭ ăr′ĭd) 10 — poor, dry land.

sheik (shēk) 12 — the chief of an Arabian tribe.

tenant (tĕn′ănt) farmer 49 — men who rent the farms on which they work from landowners.

Pronouncing Index